Are

Your

Health and Finances

Linked?

A Christian Entrepreneur's Quest

Ruth Wuwong

Disclaimer Notice:

Please note the information contained within this document is for educational and entertainment purposes only. All effort has been executed to present accurate, up-to-date, reliable, complete information. No warranties of any kind are declared or implied. Readers acknowledge the author is not engaged in the rendering of legal, financial, medical, or professional advice.
Under no circumstances will any blame or legal responsibility be held against the author for any damages, reparation, or monetary loss because of the information in this booklet directly or indirectly.

Unless otherwise noted, all Scripture taken from the New International Version.

ISBN: 979-8-88904-000-2

Published by Vidasym Publishing
A Division of Vidasym, Inc.
5013 S. Louis Ave., #532
Sioux Falls, SD 57108

DEDICATION

I dedicate this book foremost to my Savior,
the Lord Jesus Christ.

Furthermore, I dedicate this book to my friends
who have supported us
in our ministry over the years.

ENDORSEMENT

This is an easy read on health and finances. The first part is on health issues, while the second part is about finances. The author is a successful entrepreneur, a committed Christian, and a pastor's wife. I must congratulate her for writing such a useful and timely booklet on managing health and wealth. As a cardiologist, I can say for a fact that her genetic profile placed her at extremely high risk for cardiovascular disease. Yet she is in her sixties and remains healthy. This undoubtedly is because of the healthy lifestyle secrets that she shares in this booklet. Even if you only follow some of her tips, you will improve your health by leaps and bounds. Looking after one's health is vital. Managing one's finances is equally important. If you are a Christian, you should always seek first the kingdom of God and His righteousness, and all the other things will be added to you. I recommend this book to anyone who cares about keeping medical and financial health out of the ICU.

(Dr. Andrew C S Koh, writer, publisher, blogger, a retired cardiologist)

Ruth Wuwong has written a valuable booklet about living a godly life by balancing the tangible and intangible assets God has given each Christian. She begins by giving advice on preventing and managing heath concerns, those intangibles that can create or destroy a life. As a biochemist, she has a unique knowledge base on how to choose which medications and actions to take to mitigate disease and lifestyle issues. In addition, her MBA allows her the ability to balance tangible monetary assets and give financial advice to others. *Are Health and Finances Linked? A Christian Entrepreneur's Quest* is a valuable read to motivate Christians to take control of areas of their life they may often leave to chance.

(Diane E. Tatum, BS-Business Administration, Accounting, MA Teaching-Language Arts.)

Contents

FOREWORD

Who doesn't want to be successful in managing their health and finances? Christians are called to care about both. In this booklet, Ruth Wuwong provides valuable and practical advice based on her life experience and converts many of her lessons learned into habits that can be adopted to improve one's health and financial well-being. Ruth details her faith journey and its impact on critical decisions that have helped, by God's grace, to bring her and her husband Ken good health and financial security.

(Dr. Terry Opgenorth worked at Abbott Laboratories' Pharma division (now AbbVie) as scientist and executive for 20 years. After Abbott, he served as CEO of Vidasym, a start-up biotech company, and was a co-founder of VetDC, a veterinary oncology company.)

Chapter 1: Introduction

While I was a graduate student at Ohio State University, Lily took care of me like her own sister. Although Covid-19 still prevented people from traveling freely, I told my husband Ken, "Lily is in her eighties. We ought to make a special trip to see her."

A visit to this old friend brought back many recollections, some painful, some sweet. During our time together, Lily talked about our shared past. "I remember your father passed away when you were sixteen. Your mother once mentioned to me you have a bad family history of high cholesterol, diabetes, and weight issues. I noticed your mother was overweight and had diabetes. Back then, even at the tender age of twenty, you appeared rather chubby."

She grasped my hand, her lips curling into a grin. "Look at you now. You're in your late sixties, right? You're slim and robust. What did you do to overcome your genetic predispositions, even when the statistics aren't in your favor? You should share your tips. I'm sure others will benefit from them."

Her words triggered such intense emotions that I became tongue-tied. Memories of my entire lifetime crashed over me, leaving one truth in their wake—God has guided us through insurmountable challenges to reach our current status, not only with my health but also with wealth and good relationships.

My husband, Ken, is a retired pastor, and together, he and I served at three different churches from 1987 to 2020. During that time, we counseled quite a few couples, and I made an interesting observation. Financial anxieties hurt health and relationships. The reverse is also true. Poor relationships affect people's well-being and prevent them from pursuing their dreams, and illness disrupts marriage and a person's pursuit of financial independence. Health, wealth, and relationships intertwine so intimately that it is difficult to single any of them out.

No, we aren't wealthy like Bill Gates or Warren Buffett, but have achieved financial independence. When we got married, the combined dollar amount in our checking account was less than fifty dollars. Yet we've come a long way! We can retire early on our own terms and donate sizeable sums of money to selected nonprofit organizations.

In the following chapters, I hope my shared stories will help you improve your health and wealth.

Chapter 2: My Body, My Health

If one million—1,000,000—represents your life, your health is the number **One** that is followed by many zeros, with each zero representing one of your treasured things. Without that One, all those zeros amount to nothing.

We all know health is important. Many of us spend money and effort trying to maintain our well-being: avoid tobacco/drug usage, reduce alcohol intake, build our diet around healthy choices, exercise, get enough sleep… The list can be long.

But how do we define good health? If I don't have any disease or infirmity, am I considered a healthy person?

Although different definitions have been used to define "health" for distinct purposes, information from the World Health Organization (WHO) shows that health is a state of complete physical, mental, and social well-being and not merely the absence of disease and infirmity. Furthermore, health is a positive concept emphasizing social and personal resources, as well as physical capacities.

Data from the Centers for Disease Control and Prevention (CDC) show that healthcare costs in the United States were $3.5 trillion in 2017. Yet we have a lower life expectancy than people in other developed countries.

Why?

There are no straightforward answers.

Although physical condition comes to mind automatically when we mention the word *health*, spiritual, relational, and financial aspects are equally important. Many studies have shown these different components intertwine and affect one another in a profound way.

For example, people with better relationships have a larger capacity to handle hardship and suffering and achieve better emotional balance. Those with good spiritual health may feel a sense of calm and purpose that drives them to achieve harmony in other aspects of life.

So, what contributes to good physical health? The cliché response is to establish healthy habits in your diet, exercise, and sleep.

My stories begin with a question that seeks a quick response, but unfortunately, there is no such thing as an easy answer. Read on to find out how I came up with workable solutions for my health issues.

Chapter 3: Establish Healthy Habits

Most of us brush our teeth every day. How did we form that habit? Likely, our parents imposed it on us before we learned that teeth brushing is important for maintaining oral hygiene.

We all know diet and exercise are crucial for better physical health. Yet, why do many of us find it difficult to eat right and exercise every day? Why can't we make them as easy as brushing our teeth?

In my early forties, an annual physical checkup revealed I had high cholesterol and that my HbA1c (a measure of average blood glucose sugar levels for the last two to three months) trended high.

My doctor advised me to change my eating habit and lose weight. "Do you exercise regularly? A combination of exercise and diet will help." Then she sent me to a dietitian.

I still remember the dietitian's earnest countenance when she stared into my eyes. "You can't eat out anymore. When you cook your meals, avoid meat and seafood high in cholesterol such as shrimp and squid."

Her words spiraled my spirit into despair, for I love food. My husband would often joke that I thought about what to eat for dinner right after I finished lunch.

During the previous twenty years, my life had formed a routine that seemed to serve me well. How could I alter it?

The answer stared back at me—my routine didn't work anymore. If I didn't change, soon the combined genetic predispositions of high cholesterol and diabetes would wreck my health. My father died young, so I didn't know whether he'd developed hyperlipidemia. But all my uncles and aunts suffered dire consequences such as stroke or heart attack from high cholesterol. On my mother's side, complications associated with obesity and diabetes killed my grandfather and one of her siblings. My mom was also overweight and diabetic. Eventually, she passed away from a diabetes-induced stroke.

Yet, what could I do to change my diet and start exercising?

As a scientist with a PhD in biochemistry, I approach everything by first conducting thorough research. I tried to learn as much as I could about diet and exercise and found something interesting: Most people fail because they don't realize that the only way to eat right and exercise consistently is to turn them into habits. For example, once you form the habit of exercise, and it becomes like brushing your teeth in the morning, you'll have a better chance of adhering to it.

So, I delved deeper into the subject of how to form a habit.

Some of you may have heard about the 21-day habit formation formula. However, according to Dr. Phillippa Lally, a health psychology researcher at University College London, a new habit may take over two months to take shape and more than eight months to become fully formed.

No wonder it's so challenging for us to establish an exercise routine.

In his book, *The Power of Habit*, Charles Duhigg attributes the formation of habits to a psychological pattern called the "habit loop"—the trigger (or cue), the routine, and the reward.

Studies have shown that an effective way to shift a habit is to discover and keep your old cue and reward and change only the routine.

From my personal experiences, I concur with that approach.

First, I dissected my daily routine.

For years, I have been following the No-B-No-B (No-Bible-No-Breakfast) practice for my daily devotion. Here is the cue-routine-reward loop associated with that habit.

Cue: My alarm goes off at 6 a.m.

Routine: I get up, brush my teeth, wash my face, and then do my morning devotion.

Reward: I'm mentally calm and prepared to start a new day. Also, now I get to eat my breakfast.

What should I do to modify my routine and to keep the same cue and reward?

Now, please note another word of caution: **DO NOT** try to change your routine all at once. Instead, take baby steps to insert small, achievable activities into that routine. Otherwise, you're doomed to fail.

After some consideration, I added ten simple sit-ups following my prayer.

Good gracious, not as easy as I thought!

In my hurry to get to breakfast and dash out of the door for work, I had to force myself to get it done. As time went by, the new mini-habit stuck, and I added additional stretch exercises and even foot massage (reflexology: see Chapter 4 for more information). In all, I only added ten more minutes to my routine. I have been doing this for 20+ years and truly benefit from my habitual morning exercise.

Yet I needed thirty minutes of exercise each day, including a good cardiovascular workout.

Back to Square One. I observed that after work, I picked up my son from school, went home, and then took a shower as if to wash away all my anxieties and worries brought on by my job.

Here is another cue-routine-reward loop associated with that habit.

Cue: I get home and drop my purse on the sofa.

Routine: I take a shower.

Reward: I feel refreshed and ready to cook dinner.

Could I exercise before taking a shower? Why not?

Again, I started small. From an extensive online search, I concluded that rope-jumping, which does not require a lot of space and investment, should be something to try. Plus, it offers numerous other benefits. Besides providing an efficient cardio workout, it also enhances balance and agility and boosts bone density.

On the first day, I jumped ten times and was already huffing and puffing as if I'd just run a marathon. Well, I had not skipped rope since middle school. I decided on the spot to cut it down and jump only five times. From that humble beginning, things got better. Still, it took me an entire year to increase to 300 times. Later, I broke the 300 times into five cycles and added stretching and weight-lifting in between.

In essence, I added only twenty more minutes to my routine and have gained tremendous benefits. I reached the goal of bringing my body mass index (BMI) into the standard range. Not only do I feel stronger and more energetic, but I have been maintaining the same BMI for the past two decades.

Enough about exercise. How about food—an entirely different beast?

As mentioned above, I love food. I've tried dieting to no avail. When I'm hungry, I tend to eat whatever I can get my hands on. After reflecting on my eating habit, I decided to eat more often in small portions. In other words, avoid getting into a food-craving state at all costs.

I discovered that besides three meals, my daily routine involved two coffee breaks, one in the morning at around 10 a.m. and the other at 3 p.m.

Here is the cue-routine-reward loop associated with that habit.

Cue: I glance at my watch. 10 a.m. Time for my coffee break.

Routine: I get up, grab a cup of coffee, and then snatch a piece of whatever sweets provided by my company on that day.

Reward: I feel relaxed, satisfied, and ready to get back to work.

Should I bring my own healthier choices and enjoy them during the coffee break?

So, I maintained the same cue/reward and replaced the routine with an apple or a banana instead of sweets. Gradually, I establish my current habit of eating six times a day.

Breakfast (around 7 a.m.): low carbs like a 1/2 cup serving of cottage cheese, or one medium avocado, or a cup of smoothie made from veggies and fruits.

Mid-morning snack (around 10 a.m.): fruit or yogurt.

Lunch (around noon): some carbs like noodles or pasta, plus an egg and vegetables.

Mid-afternoon snack (around 3 p.m.): fruit or yogurt.

Dinner (around 6 p.m.): no carbs, meat and vegetables only.

Night-time snack (around 9 p.m.): fruit.

By eating frequent small portions, my blood glucose and insulin levels won't spike and fall into a wild pattern. My mother developed full-blown diabetes in her forties. As of today (in my late sixties), I have managed to fend it off. I believe weight control, diet, exercise, and foot massage (see Chapter 4) all help.

Another reminder: Avoid processed food. If possible, try to make everything from scratch, which is healthier and more economical.

As mentioned above, I often eat cottage cheese for breakfast, but it's plain, almost tasteless. To make it more appetizing, I used to mix jam into it, even though commercially prepared jam contains a high percentage of added sugars.

Could I replace the jam from the store with something homemade?

At the end of one summer, I found hundreds of unripe fruits on the cherry tomato vines in my garden.

Should I dump them? What a waste.

After some research, I made them into a smoothie, then boiled it with sugar and maltose (for thickening). The product? A homemade green sauce perfect for my cottage cheese. Since I added little sugar with no preservatives, I froze them into small Ziplock bags and thawed one bag each week. If you're interested in the recipe, drop me a note, and I'll send it to you.

So far, I have only talked about good habits. What about if you have bad habits such as smoking, drugs, or alcohol? Can you break unhealthy habits by following the same cue-routine-reward loop?

Yes, and no. Some problems require professional help and are beyond the scope of this book.

I do recommend, if possible, joining an accountability group.

For several months, I belonged to an accountability group at our church. The four of us, all women, met once a week.

Initially, we focused on reporting what we did during the past week, including whether we read our Bible daily, exercised, and ate a healthy diet. The sharing helped us recognize our bad habits, and we encouraged one another to establish healthy ones.

Our small group soon morphed beyond health issues. When we grew more intimate, we shared our problems concerning work, spouses, children, etc. One of the sisters back then faced a dilemma: whether to pursue her PhD degree in theology. With the help of the accountability group, she reached her decision. A few weeks ago, she sent me a message to thank me for my encouragement and informed me she is now a Doctor of Old Testament Theology and a regular speaker at various events.

I hope my sharing convinces you it's possible to form a daily habit of eating right and exercising. You may even go beyond that and receive your PhD in theology.

Chapter 4: Reflexology and the Benefits of Foot Massage

As a biochemist trained in the Western scientific tradition, I used to object to anything related to Chinese medicine and alternative healing, until a trip to Shanghai changed my perspective.

During a visit to our family in Hong Kong a few years ago, we detoured to mainland China, which had just opened to tourists. While our tour group went to Shanghai, one of my teeth began to give me trouble. The pain became more intolerable by the minute. To our surprise, a sign advertised that a doctor specializing in reflexology resided within our hotel.

"I'll give it a try," I muttered to Ken, gritting my teeth in agony. "It can't get any worse, anyway."

I entered the doctor's office and caught sight of a large, middle-aged woman sitting alone. She gave me a questioning glance but didn't utter a word.

"I—I—" I spoke in Mandarin and grimaced with wry amusement, feeling foolish.

"Can I help you?" Her voice was gentle, unlike her impressive frame.

I swallowed my embarrassment. "I'm here for my toothache."

She gestured for me to take a seat. "Please remove your shoes and socks."

I did as she commanded. She wiped my right foot thoroughly with alcohol and pressed along the length of my sole. At one spot, she paused and raised her head. "You had bronchitis recently?"

My jaw almost dropped to the floor. *How did she know?*

She moved to my other foot. After a moment, she looked at me again. "You have a diabetic family background."

I couldn't control my curiosity anymore. "You can tell from examining my feet?"

"Yes." She uttered one simple response and went back to work. "Which tooth is giving you trouble?"

I opened my mouth and pointed to the culprit.

She nodded. "Be prepared. As I press hard on one of your toes, it'll hurt like crazy, but your toothache will subside."

Serious doubts crept into my mind. Then she pushed down on the second toe of my right foot, and I almost jumped up from the chair.

"How does your tooth feel?" she asked in a calm and kind tone.

Tears gathered behind my eyelids. I didn't know if the pain in my toe distracted me or if my toothache had disappeared. "It worked."

"Good. The pain will return, though. Next time when it starts, just massage this point." She showed me the exact spot on my toe. "By the way, you can delay the onset of diabetes by pressing here." She pointed to a small area on my sole.

I walked out of her office, bewilderment bubbling up in my heart. As I entered our room, I couldn't help blurting out, "Ken, you wouldn't believe what I've experienced."

After I told him the story, he shook his head. "I don't believe it. It sounds like magic."

I crossed my arms. "Why don't you go check it out yourself?"

"But I'm not sick." He scratched his head. "Did you say it only cost twenty Chinese yuan? Well, that's not even five US dollars. I'll go."

Thirty minutes later, Ken returned with a disbelieving expression on his face. "She studied my feet and told me I had appendicitis before. She also asked me why I wanted to see her since my health is excellent."

Astonishing, isn't it? Do a Google search, and you'll find over 485,000,000 results on this subject. You can easily purchase a simple foot massage tool for a few bucks. Some books give elaborate illustrations about where to massage, etc. I think the simplest way is to massage your whole foot, bottom, top, and toes. If you make it too complicated, you'll give it up sooner or later. Keep it simple and make it a daily habit.

Since my encounter with that amazing doctor, I've been massaging my feet every morning. My mother had her diabetic onset in her forties. I passed that age more than two decades ago and still haven't developed diabetes. Maybe foot massage does delay the onset of that horrid disease.

Chapter 5: Vitamin D

Have you seen the article entitled "How Vitamin D Affects Omicron Symptoms?" If interested, please drop me a note on my website, www.ruthforchrist.com, and I'll send you the report.

Here is a paragraph from that commentary:

"There may be an association of low vitamin D levels correlated with severe diseases, COVID-19 included. But if there is an immune-boosting benefit to be had, 'it is with standard, low doses and not large doses,' Dr. Spearman clarifies."

About twenty years ago, I started to conduct research in the vitamin D field and quickly learned that my daily intake of 400 IU of vitamin D wasn't sufficient. So, I increased it to 1000 IU a day.

Imagine my shock when my doctor told me I was vitamin D deficient. I didn't have any symptoms other than that my joints hurt sometimes, and I was prone to mild colds. My doctor gave me a prescription for a mega 50,000 IU dose. I took the prescription from her but didn't fill it. Why? Because I knew the hypercalcemic side effect of vitamin D overdose would be detrimental to my body. Instead, I raised my daily intake to 2000 IU. It worked. My vitamin D level went back to normal, and I no longer suffered from joint pain and frequent mild cold.

Is vitamin D a vitamin?

Most people may respond, "Of course."

Yet, the correct answer may surprise you.

13

Many of us know that vitamin D is made in the skin after exposure to sunshine. But the initial form is inactive. It needs to be chemically changed in the liver and kidney in order to become the active form, calcitriol.

Like estrogen or androgen, calcitriol is a hormone that binds to a nuclear receptor, the vitamin D receptor (VDR). Once bound, calcitriol activates VDR to regulate over 200 target genes.

The fact that vitamin D is essential for bone health is well known. Additional evidence suggests that VDR plays an important role in modulating cardiovascular, immunological, metabolic, and other functions. For example, data from epidemiological, preclinical, and clinical studies show that vitamin D deficiency is associated with an increased risk for cardiovascular disease.

Thus, the benefits of vitamin D go beyond building and maintaining strong bones and teeth. To improve your overall health, remember to take 2000 IU of vitamin D every day.

Chapter 6: Stress and Lack of Sleep

Stress can wreak havoc on your mind and body, affecting your sleep, diet, or even your exercise routine. Some specific events in life, such as moving to a new place, changing jobs, or losing a loved one, often lead to increased stress. In our daily routine, do we also experience stress? How do we recognize it?

Several years ago, I worked as a project manager for a major pharmaceutical company. My workload increased bit by bit. Soon, I kept thinking about my job even at night and developed insomnia. My body needed rest, but my mind didn't want to cooperate. I tossed and turned like the sea. Yet no matter how hard I tried, I couldn't sleep. Then the morning came, and I still had to drag my sleep-deprived body to work.

If you have ever experienced sleepless nights, you know how awful it is.

Information from the American Academy of Sleep Medicine website shows that about a third of Americans suffer from periodic insomnia. When you have difficulty sleeping for more than a month, it turns into a chronic condition. One in ten of us may have this chronic disorder and require treatment.

Many factors (e.g., aging, caffeine, pain, medications, apnea, and stress) contribute to insomnia. Stress affects sleep. On the other hand, insomnia also causes stress. It's a vicious cycle.

After I pinned down stress as the reason for my chronic insomnia,

I asked several people, "What should I do?"

"Quit your job," one woman from my church quipped.

Sorry, not an option.

Another Christian gave me a hard glance. "Have more faith. Pray and leave everything to the Lord."

A friend suggested, "Drink a glass of wine in the evening. It'll make you sleepy."

I did an online search and learned that alcohol may make you feel sleepy at first. But as the alcohol is metabolized, it'll disrupt your sleep. A study shows two drinks for men and one drink for women can decrease sleep quality by 24 percent.

I considered asking my doctor for sleeping pills. With three decades of experiences in the pharmaceutical industry, defaulting to medication seemed an easy way out. Yet, after suffering unwanted effects from certain drugs for years (see Chapter 8 for more information), I've developed a unique concept: Unless it's absolutely necessary, avoid medications.

One day during my morning devotion, I brought my problem to the Lord again, and an idea popped into my mind. "Find a hobby that lets you use your hands, not your brain."

Ah, that was exactly what I needed.

After investigating different hobbies, I settled on jewelry making, mainly because it didn't require a lot of space. I went to a community college to take a course. Every evening at around nine o'clock, I pushed aside my work and focused on my crafts. Amazingly, when I kept my hands busy, my mind automatically relaxed. In a short while, I overcame my insomnia.

Besides having a hobby, other approaches such as exercise, meditation, yoga, massage, etc. can all help reduce stress. However, inactive ways of passing time, such as watching television or surfing the internet, may increase your stress level over the long run.

So, focus on using active methods to manage your stress.

Regarding how to build a better sleep habit, you can find numerous helpful articles by researching the subject on the internet. Follow the cue-routine-reward approach I discussed in Chapter 3, and you may overcome your insomnia.

When you try all sorts of strategies and still experience stress and insomnia almost daily, what should you do? It's time to see a doctor.

Last, I would like to share a self-hypnosis method of falling asleep that my husband learned in a workshop on "Hypnosis" years ago. It traced back to the training program of the US military. Understandably, soldiers have to adapt to various situations and need to fall asleep fast. They must get enough rest so that they can perform tasks once they wake up. My husband has used it for many years, and it's very effective.

From a medical point of view, hypnosis is a form of psychological therapy. It's intended under professional supervision to change the state of awareness by relaxing the body to improve focus and concentration. This differs from the portrayal of hypnosis in popular culture, where the hypnotized person loses control, and his behavior is manipulated by another person. Although the second form of hypnosis has statistical data to explain its phenomena, conclusive results from scientific research are lacking.

Self-hypnosis to fall asleep is just one application using the principle of hypnosis. It relies on one's own will and imagination, leading to the desired goal of falling asleep fast.

In practice, we first lie flat on the bed, ensuring there are enough blankets after we fall asleep. Then we learn to lie still and relax the muscles of the whole body. Starting from the top of the head, we check if our face is relaxed. If we are unsure, the easiest way is to tighten our eyes and mouth, then loosen them up slowly. Afterwards, we move on to the neck and shoulder. We check on the fingers. Any tense areas need to be loosened and remain relaxed.

The second step is to imagine a machine that scans from head to toe, and you, like a bystander, trace the scanning beam. During the scan, you keep breathing slowly and deeply. Imagine that the beam is moving downward, from the forehead, eyebrows, eyes, bridge of the nose, lips... If you realize the beam has missed a part, backtrack and continue. You can always start it all over. After it passes the neck, let it do the left arm first, all the way to the tip of every finger. Let it return to the neck and do the right arm. Let it go back again and continue down the body. In such a manner, you have it scan the whole body. Whenever you are distracted, tell yourself not to think but to focus on the body. The entire body can be scanned at a normal speed in two or three minutes. Repeat the process if you are still awake. After you practice this regularly, you can fall asleep quickly.

I once did a comparison in winter. On the first night, I wanted to lie down and fall asleep naturally. My hands and feet began to warm up after 20 minutes. The next night, I used self-hypnosis and imagine that there was a warm spring flowing through my body. Within three minutes, my body warmed up. I didn't understand why, but it worked.

Being unable to fall asleep is frustrating. Whatever method we use, we must first determine that we "need" adequate sleep for health reasons and for functioning properly the next day. Self-hypnosis cannot guarantee that you'll fall asleep. Since a lot of research has been done about this method, you should at least give it a try, which is better than tossing and turning in bed for a long time.

Chapter 7: Regular Checkups

When I reached age fifty, our insurance policy covered colonoscopy, a procedure that allows the doctor to examine the large bowel and the distal part of the small bowel by a scope with a camera.

The procedure itself isn't painful because you usually don't feel anything after the sedative injection. However, the preparation beforehand is daunting for it involves: (1) eating low-fiber foods for three days, (2) going on a clear liquid diet one day before, and (3) drinking a prescription laxative drink to clean out the bowel.

I debated whether to have it done.

Should I do it? None of my family members has a history of colon cancer.

On the other hand, the anesthesia-related risk and some discomfort shouldn't deter me from an insurance-covered procedure, right?

At last, I mustered up my courage and made an appointment.

The doctor removed a large polyp packed with cancer cells!

Unlike most people who undergo colonoscopy once every 5-10 years, I went through it three times that year since my doctor worried the cancer cells might have escaped from the polyp into surrounding areas. Fortunately, the two follow-up procedures didn't detect any sign of cancer.

My primary care physician told me, "You're a lucky lady. They caught it in the nick of time."

I believe everybody will benefit from regular checkups. I also learned about my cholesterol and glucose problems through my annual physical, which led me to alter my diet and add exercise to my daily routine (see Chapter 3).

Besides the insurance-covered preventive care in the US, a few years ago, we took a medical trip to Taiwan. Several hospitals in Taiwan, including the famous Taipei Veterans General Hospital, offer a whole-body-MRI-for-tumor screening (GI tract not included) at NT$42,000 (equivalent to about $1,400). We paid less than $1,000 back in 2011. As a comparison, the average cost of a *localized* MRI in the US is about $1,300.

During that trip, the results turned out well for me and my husband. However, they found my cousin had early-stage prostate cancer. Even scarier, one of our friends had pancreatic cancer. Neither of them had symptoms nor felt any discomfort. After returning to the US, our friend went to his doctor right away. He had another MRI done for the pancreas, which confirmed pancreatic cancer. Then, he scheduled an appointment with an oncologist. Following the surgery, the doctor commented, "In my 20+ years as a surgeon, I've never caught pancreatic cancer at such an early stage. You must be doing something right."

After our friend told him about his medical trip to Taiwan, the doctor said, "Thank you for sharing this piece of information. I'm going to make a special trip there."

What happened to my cousin's prostate cancer? His story went equally well. He caught it so early that the doctor was able to give him proper treatment.

As of today, both of them are still cancer-free.

So, besides regular checkups in the US, if you can, you might consider taking your next vacation in Taiwan for a whole-body MRI screening. It may even save your life.

Chapter 8: Know Your Pills

The Food and Drug Administration (FDA) first allowed emergency use of the Pfizer–BioNTech vaccine on December 10, 2020, to fight against COVID-19. Yet in August 2022, the report on https://usafacts.org/ showed the following national vaccination rate: 78% of the population have received at least one dose and 66% are considered fully vaccinated.

Why do people hesitate to receive the vaccine? Numerous reasons exist. Many excellent studies and articles dealt with this subject. One of those reasons has to do with the fact that people tend to lump vaccines together with medications and resist them because of perceived risks.

I understand their concerns. I've been working in the pharmaceutical industry all my life and have interacted with the FDA for quite a few years. A new prescription drug must go through five steps:

1. Discovery/concept: For example, someone in a company comes up with an idea of developing a new drug to treat diabetes. They go ahead and synthesize novel compounds.

2. Preclinical research: Evaluate the compounds in test tubes and animal disease models to ensure their safety and effectiveness.

3. Clinical research: Select one lead compound and evaluate it in human clinical studies to confirm its safety and effectiveness. Submit the results to the FDA.

21

4. FDA review/approval: The FDA follows a rigorous evaluation process to determine whether a drug provides benefits that outweigh its known and potential risks for the intended population.

5. Post-market safety monitoring: Continue to track the drug's safety and effectiveness in patients.

The above information probably has already given you a subtle cue that all medicines can cause side effects. My knowledge in the field led me to develop a philosophy: Don't take medications unless necessary.

Yet, sooner or later, most of us will run into a situation in which we have no choice. My time came shortly after I reached forty. That year's annual physical checkup revealed I had high cholesterol (total cholesterol, 342; LDL, the bad cholesterol, 267; HDL, the good cholesterol, less than 10; triglycerides, 187).

My primary care physician, Dr. Stone, gave me a stern warning. "You need to diet and exercise so that you can control your total cholesterol to be <200, LDL at <100, and triglycerides at <149. Also, your HDL must be higher than 50."

Although I knew well only about 20% of the cholesterol in my bloodstream came from food and my body made the rest, I took her advice and started a stringent routine of diet and exercise.

Three months later, nothing improved, and Dr. Stone prescribed Lipitor. The most serious side effect of Lipitor is myopathy, a dysfunction of the muscle fibers. In a few weeks, I developed severe muscle aches, and my doctor put me on Vytorin.

Everything went well until I failed to get up one morning. My whole body hurt as if a high fever had hit me. Dr. Stone sent me to see a cardiologist right away because she worried the drug might have damaged my heart muscle. Luckily, a stress test revealed my heart function had not decreased.

Back to square one. Dr. Stone stared into my eyes. "I'm giving you the five-milligram Crestor, the lowest dose. If you develop side effects, I don't know what else to give you."

Again, everything seemed well. I told my husband, "Finally, something works for me."

Then, one day, my son Jon grasped my right palm, and I shrieked with pain.

Jon stared at me with concern. "Are you okay?"

I checked the area below my ring finger. It appeared swollen. Had

I bumped into something? I didn't remember injuring it.

During the next few days, the lump grew so big that I could no longer close my hand to make a fist.

Back in Dr. Stone's office, I gazed at my hand and wondered what went wrong with my health. She examined the swelling. "I'll send you to an orthopedic surgeon right away."

Dr. Philips, the orthopedic surgeon, checked the X-ray pictures. "Looks like a badly inflamed tendon."

"How can it be? I haven't had any accidents or injuries." I scratched my forehead.

"Repetitive motions can also cause it." He surveyed the films again. "You have a few choices: physical therapy, medications, cortisone shots, or surgery."

I opted for the first.

Three weeks later, my condition became so severe that even picking up a teacup turned into a challenge. My physical therapist gave up. "It's not working at all. You need more aggressive treatment."

I returned to Dr. Philips. He examined my boxing glove-like hand with obvious sympathy in his eyes. "I'll give you an injection today. Be prepared. It'll be the worst shot you've ever had in your life. Afterward, the inflammation will subside."

He numbed the area before sticking the needle into the gap between my fingers. I gritted my teeth. Excruciating pain shot through my hand and up every nerve into my shoulder.

Within a week, the swelling on my hand went down, but I found two more bumps on my left arm. This time, I reached my conclusion—the side effect of Crestor. With Dr. Stone's permission, I stopped taking the statin for two months. My tendon problem eased. Unfortunately, my cholesterol went back to over 300. Dr. Stone warned me, "You must go back on Crestor. Although tendonitis is painful, at least it won't kill you."

Back to my research mode. I found a CardioChek Analyzer lipid profile kit on Amazon to monitor my total cholesterol, HDL, and triglyceride levels at home and conducted a one-person clinical study on myself. I found that by taking one milligram of Crestor, I could control my parameters without the problem of tendon inflammation.

Later, I shared my experience with several friends, which prompted them to re-evaluate their pills. One of them told me recently, "I cut my Lipitor in half. Not only is my cholesterol still less than 200, I no longer feel weak and groggy every day. Thank you for alerting me about the side effect of my medication."

So, if you find your hair falling out in clumps, check whether your pills are causing it. Many common medications, such as those for high blood pressure, psoriasis, and arthritis, are linked to hair loss. And if you take pills to prevent osteoporosis, be aware that long-term bisphosphonate therapy has been linked to a type of thigh fracture called an atypical femoral fracture. Nearly half of the adult population in the US has high blood pressure. Are you one of them? If so, watch out for medications (anti-inflammatory drugs such as ibuprofen, certain antidepressants, and oral steroids) that undermine the effectiveness of your hypertension meds.

I usually read the package insert for my medications, which lists numerous potential side effects. If you don't have the training to understand it, seek help from your pharmacists or friends. Spending time and effort to learn more about your medications will do you a lot of good in the long run.

Chapter 9: Depression

As Christians, no matter what happens, we should always express joy and gratitude toward God to serve as powerful witnesses for Jesus. Right?

Devout Christians who suffer from depression may feel ashamed to tell others because they blame it on their lack of faith in God's healing power. If I prayed more, trusted God more, and read my Bible more, would the depression go away? Yet, my own experiences tell me those so-called "religious activities" seldom help. For total healing, we must acknowledge that faithful followers of Jesus Christ do fall into depression.

So far, research still hasn't pinned down the exact causes of depression. You can find information about potential factors on trustworthy websites (e.g., the Mayo Clinic website).

My depression began after my mother passed away. I've written about that part of my life in a book entitled *The Way We Forgive* (under my pen name, R. F. Whong). Below is an excerpt.

> *Many nights I lay awake. Faint noises from the hallway roused my hopes. Mom's shuffling to the bathroom. As I came back to my senses, I couldn't help but burst into tears. She'd never live with us again.*
>
> *Sympathetic words from others just brought more misery. Like the prophet Elijah, I pleaded with God, "Enough.*

Everything under the sun is meaningless. Please take away my life."

Yes, feelings of sadness and hopelessness accompanied me every minute. I experienced a sleep disturbance. Remorse and guilt filled my soul with questions such as, "Would Mom still be around if I'd only done…"

I couldn't function like before and had difficulty concentrating and making decisions.

Several times on the highway, I fought the temptation to swerve my car to the opposite lane. The only thing that held me back was my mother's words, "Live, and live an abundant life as our Lord Jesus has promised us."

The weird fact was that I didn't want to seek medical help.

My husband, a trained professional counselor, recognized my symptoms. Still, he couldn't make me go to my doctor and could only ask brothers and sisters from church to pray for me.

I visited the library and read many books about death and near-death experience. By God's grace, certain articles pointed me toward a potential source of my problems. After my dad passed away when I was sixteen, I didn't have the luxury of processing my grief properly because my aunt, whom I've loved since childhood, kicked my mom and me out of our shared house. The unresolved grief, along with my aunt's betrayal, injured my soul. Throughout my life, I worked hard to suppress my hurt. After becoming a Christian, I felt ashamed of my fear of death and my resentment toward my aunt. I became a control freak in vain attempts to exert power over the uncontrollable.

Since Mom's death was beyond my control, I spiraled into depression.

The final breakthrough came one morning as I kneeled before the Lord and cried out, "Did You walk with my mother when she traversed the valley of death?"

"Yes, I did." A clear message popped into my head. I shot up to my feet, goose bumps crawling all over my body.

From that day on, I gradually emerged from my cocoon of despair.

During that difficult period, my husband played a crucial role in my recovery. In addition, my own prayers and the prayers of others helped sustain me. I'm convinced the power of prayer is beyond human comprehension.

Everybody's situation is unique. My depression was situational, and with the support of friends and family members, my recovery was possible once I came to terms with my mother's death. With a chronic depressive disorder, although its cause isn't fully understood, disturbances in the levels of certain chemicals, such as neurotransmitters, may be the culprit. Some will need to see a doctor and take medications.

I should offer one piece of advice from my experience: You can't be alone in depression. You need to have someone by your side to support you. If you don't have family members around you, reach out to trusted individuals in your faith community.

Last but not least, be assured that God, the Almighty Healer, will walk with you through the deepest, darkest valleys.

Chapter 10: About Money

When I studied at the University of Illinois for my MBA in finance, I learned something crucial, not from my textbooks but from a professor's comment. "Making money is important, but how to manage what you have is even more critical."

Financial health depends on what you do in both areas.

All too often, we hear about big lottery winners who later lost it all.

I read this piece of news online some time ago with interest. "Five years after a Kentucky resident won a $27 million jackpot, he was penniless and living in a storage shed with his wife. The couple squandered their fortune on the typical goodies that sink so many lucky winners. They bought dozens of high-end cars, mansions, and a plane…"

In my mind, managing my money takes precedence over bringing in new money. In this booklet, I'll share my tips on the management side and also touch upon investment.

Some questions may pop up at the mention of investment.

Should Christians invest in the stock market? Is it like gambling? What does the Bible teach about investing?

Remember Jesus' parable about the three servants and their given talents? In Matthew 25:14-30, Jesus talked about a man who, before he left for a trip, summoned his three servants and entrusted them with talents in various amounts according to their abilities. The first two individuals doubled their money, while the third person dug a hole in the ground and hid his talent. When the master returned, he gave the third servant a hard time.

People often ask, "What did the third servant do wrong? Wasn't it the right thing to do to keep the master's entrusted treasure safe by burying it? Why did he get reprimanded? What would the master say if the other two invested and lost their money?"

My reply below is based on my understanding of God's attributes. The master had the entire world under his sovereignty. Loss or gain wasn't his primary concern. What he wanted from the three servants was their obedience to his command to make good use of what they had. Risks and challenges are critical ingredients of the abundant life that the Lord has promised us.

Everything, including my life, is entrusted to me temporarily. My responsibility as a manager is to well use what God has given me according to His guidance.

So, I not only invest in stocks but also trade options.

In my MBA program, I learned a lot about different techniques related to financial management, yet three key principles from my professors benefitted me more than anything else.

The first principle: The US market is very efficient. When a piece of news reaches you, likely most people have already learned about it. In other words, don't believe what others tell you about which stock to buy and don't invest in anything you don't understand.

The second principle: At any given time, the pool of money is fixed. When someone loses money, where does the money go? To another person. If you want to make money, pay attention to those who constantly lose money and try to do the opposite.

The third principle: Risks and returns always go hand-in-hand. Higher returns mean greater risk. There is no such thing as a no-risk investment. Even money in your checking/saving account, seemingly safe on the surface, encounters two risks: opportunity cost (the failure to use cash in an economically efficient way) and inflation.

As shown in the following chapters, I derive most of my practical investment strategies based on these three pieces of advice.

Chapter 11: Income, Expenses, and Personal Financial Statement

I must reiterate the advice from my professor that weighs more than gold. "Making money is important, but how to manage what you have is even more critical."

The starting point to manage your current circumstance? Conduct a thorough analysis.

In finances, that means you'll have to track income and expenses, which sounds easier than it is.

I've often served as a financial planner free of charge for people in my church. Once, a brother asked me to help him. I told him, "Okay, here's an excel sheet. Please track your income and expenses for three months, then we'll discuss how to invest."

He tried it for two weeks and gave up. Without that critical piece of information, I could do nothing for him.

You may ask, "Why three months? Do I have to do it every year? It's a pain in the neck."

What is the reason for doing it for three consecutive months? The average data after three months of tracking will provide a better understanding of your financial status because sometimes monthly income and expenses are irregular. For example, we pay our estimated tax quarterly, not monthly.

No, you don't have to do it every year. From my experiences, you should get it done every time a significant change takes place in your life that potentially affects your financial situation. For example, you move to a different city, receive an outstanding promotion, or add a child...

The table at the end of this chapter is a comprehensive list of items to track. At this point, you sigh and wonder, "Can I do it? It looks tedious and may involve a lot of work."

Remember what I discussed earlier (Chapter 3) about the "habit loop"—the trigger (or cue), the routine, and the reward?

Trust me. You can do it once you build it into a habit.

For me, I identified my journaling as the place to add this extra step into the routine. I collected all the information and receipts and simply jotted them into my diary. Then, once a week, I transferred the entries into my excel sheet, which looks exactly like the table shown at the end of this chapter, except that now I can conduct my calculation. Drop me a note on my website, and I'll email you the excel spreadsheet.

Meanwhile, put together your personal financial statement, which is a snapshot of your financial position at a specific point in time.

First step: List your assets (what you own), which include cash in CDs, checking, and saving accounts, securities such as stocks, bonds, and mutual funds, life insurance (cash surrender value), personal property (autos, jewelry, etc.), real estate (market value), and retirement funds (e.g., IRAs, 401k).

Second step: List your liabilities (what you owe), which include current debt (credit cards, loans), taxes you need to pay, real estate mortgages, etc.

Third step: Subtract liabilities from assets to get your net worth.

Like a balance sheet in a company, this should be done at least once a year.

Again, drop me a note on my website, and I'll email you an excel spreadsheet. Or, you can easily google and find a similar one.

You have taken the first step. The reward? You know your net worth and how much extra money you can pour into investment.

	Days			
1. Monthly Income	1	2	...	31
Salary				
Other pay				
Investment income				
Scholarships				
Money from other sources				
Total Income				
2. Monthly Expenses	1	2	...	31
Mortgage				
Gas/electricity/water				
Garbage				
Groceries				
Child education				
Medical expenses				
Car payment				
Car maintenance				
Gasoline				
Home maintenance				
Household items				
Health insurance				
Life insurance				
Car insurance				
Long-term care insurance				
Home/rental insurance				
Meal out (+ coffee/drinks)				
Clothing/shoes				
Cable TV				
Cell phone/phone				
Internet service				
Holidays/gifts				
Vacation/travel				
Entertainment				
Beauty parlors/grooming				
Religious/charitable				
Stationaries/postage				
Income tax/ property tax				
Other				
Total Expenses				
3. Monthly Cash Flow = Monthly Income – Monthly Expenses				

Chapter 12: Invest in Education

Before we invest in the stock market and other productive assets, I must emphasize that investing in education to broaden your knowledge will help you achieve your financial goal in the long run.

I mentioned previously that my husband, Ken, is a retired pastor, and I'm a biochemist by training. A few years after we got married, the amount in our combined checking account improved a bit, from less than fifty dollars to a few hundred dollars.

The pastor's pay wouldn't impress anyone, but it was decent. Working for a pharmaceutical company, I made twice as much as Ken. With our combined income, why did we still struggle to pay bills every month?

I realized both of us knew nothing about finances.

After many prayers, I sat my dear hubby down for a chat. "One of us must learn how to manage money. You or me? Take your pick."

The answer? Me.

Ken had no interest in money at all. Otherwise, he wouldn't have quit his civil engineer job to become a pastor.

In the beginning, I went to the library and read quite a few books about the stock market, bonds, mutual funds, etc. The more I studied, the more frustrated I felt. In the end, I concluded that if I wanted to do it right, I should try to get a complete education. So, I bit the bullet and entered the University of Illinois for my MBA degree in finance.

I must admit that those years were very challenging because I worked during the day and attended school at night. Even as an in-state student, the tuition fees became a burden. I had to forego a few "must-haves." We grew most of our vegetables in the summer, seldom ate out, and only bought second-hand furniture and cars. I learned to purchase my formal outfits (e.g., two-piece suits) at Goodwill and the Salvation Army.

After four years and about $20,000 out of my pocket, I completed the program. Boy, was it worth it!

I didn't change my career path and mainly used my knowledge to manage our own finances. And what a difference it made. In a short while, the combined number of our checking, saving, and brokerage accounts increased to more than $50,000.

Along the way, we not only learned to manage our money but also gained some precious insights.

First, owning things brings short-lived pleasure, but knowledge, like experience, stays with us for a lifetime.

Second, learning broadens our perspective and enriches our worldview. Getting skills related to your job or about how to manage money is outstanding. Yet obtaining new knowledge on various subjects (e.g., gardening, different cultures and cuisines, music appreciation, a new language, etc.) unrelated to your work can make your life more interesting and enhance your relationship with others.

Third, don't attempt to keep up with the Joneses. Stick to your principles and be content. As an example, I used to have a subordinate who drove a Mercedes. At one point, especially after we had acquired a sizable asset, I asked Ken, "Should we consider replacing our old Toyota Camry with a Mercedes?"

My wise hubby replied, "Why? Is it necessary? It's not just the upfront payment. The additional expenses, such as insurance, repairs, and maintenance, are all higher."

Yeah, he was right.

Chapter 13: Stocks and Options

Stocks: Buy Low, Sell High.

In an earlier chapter (Chapter 10), I talked about why the third servant in Jesus' parable who buried his entrusted treasure was reprimanded. I also shared that everything, including my life, is entrusted to me temporarily. My responsibility is to obey the Lord and make good use of the *talent* assigned to me according to God's guidance.

What is the key element embedded in this belief? Learn. Work hard.

If I try to invest in stocks but don't want to do research, it's gambling. Think about the fact: Professional investors have the tools, spend hours analyzing the market, and still can't make money all the time. As an amateur, how can I expect to win?

We all wish we can buy a stock at its lowest point and then sell it at its highest point.

But how?

Unfortunately, no one can provide a winning formula. However, methods exist for us to study a specific company to pin down a price range to get in and another (higher) price range to get out. I'm a lifetime member (one of my best investments) of the National Association of Investors Corp. (NAIC) and have benefited from their stock selection guide.

Interested in learning more about how to estimate future growth rates and predict a stock's potential return? You may want to check out the NAIC's website at www.betterinvesting.org.

Sell Put Options to Buy Stocks.

You have done your research and identify a few stocks you like. The only problem? According to your analysis, the stock's price is currently not in the *buy* range.

Many of you already know that you can use a limit order to buy or sell a stock at a specific price. For example, if you want to spend $90 per share to purchase shares of a $100 stock, you can set a limit order that won't be filled unless your specified price becomes available.

There is another way to do it. You can sell a put option.

What is a put option? It's <u>a contract</u> that gives the option buyer the right to sell a particular stock to you (the option seller) at a predetermined price known as the strike price, within a specified window of time. To induce you to sign the contract, the buyer will pay you an option fee, the premium, right now (i.e., the moment you sell the put).

The following is a real case study from my records.

For some time, I wanted to own a certain stock, but its price was always outside the buy range of my analysis. When the stock's price was $33, I sold five put options at a strike price of $31, with a target time of one month (i.e., the contract would expire after a month). For your information, one option is 100 shares. In another word, I entered a contract with the option buyer that he/she could force me to buy the stock at $31 one month later if the stock price fell below $31. The premium wasn't much, only $0.8/share. So, I pocketed $400 from the five puts ($0.8*500 shares = $400).

One month later, its stock price was $34. The option expired, and I didn't get to buy the stock. I still desired the stock and sold another five put options at a strike price of $33, with a target time of two months. Because this time the contract was for two months, the premium was higher at $1.6/share. I pocketed $800 ($1.6*500 shares = $800). When the option expired, I still didn't get to own the stock and sold another four rounds of put options.

The market crashed in March 2020 because of COVID-19, and that stock's price fell to $23. I was forced to buy 500 shares at $31. However, because I'd sold six rounds of puts with a cumulated premium of $8.5 per share, my actual cost to buy the stock was $22.5 ($31 minus $8.5) per share. A few months following the March 2020 market crash, the price of this stock returned to $34. By the way, this stock pays a good dividend (~$1.8 per share at ~4%), much better than the bank.

To sum up, if you have done your research and really want to own a certain stock, but its price is outside your buy range, then sell puts. If its price doesn't fall, you get to keep the premium money. If the whole market crashes because of certain disasters (e.g., COVID-19), and you're forced to purchase the stock, you'll likely own it at a discounted price.

Sell Call Options to Sell Stocks.

Although I highly recommend using the "sell-puts-to-buy-stocks" strategy, I must caution you about selling a call option to sell a stock.

Like a put option, a call option is a contract that gives the option buyer the right to buy a particular stock from you (the option seller) at a predetermined price known as the strike price, within a specified window of time. To induce you to sign the contract, the buyer will pay you an option fee, the premium, right now (i.e., the moment you sell the call).

I mentioned above that I was forced to buy a stock at $31 when its price fell to $23 in March 2020 because of COVID-19. After selling six rounds of put options with a cumulated premium of $8.5 per share, my actual cost to buy the stock is $22.5 per share, and this stock pays a decent dividend. Recently, the stock traded at around $36.

Should I sell? What do you think?

My answer is: It depends.

As an investor, generally I try to own my stocks for as long as possible, especially if the stock pays a good dividend. Under certain circumstances, however, I may need to rebalance my portfolio and will consider selling a stock.

For example, I used to work for a pharmaceutical company and received a lot of stocks as a portion of my compensation. Suddenly, I realized 50% of my entire portfolio was on that stock. Therefore, I had to diversify to reduce my exposure to risks. Let's assume that the stock price was $120. Instead of selling that stock outright, I sold five options at a strike price of $120, with a target time of one month. The premium was $3.4 per share. One month later, the stock went up to

$122 per share. I was forced to sell 500 shares at $120. However, I actually sold it for $123.4 per share.

It sounded good. The problem? That year, the capital gain put me into another tax bracket.

I would emphasize again that everything, including my life, is entrusted to me temporarily. My responsibility is to obey and be a good steward according to God's guidance. After paying a hefty tax bill that year, the Holy Spirit reminded me that owing a lot of tax because of poor planning wasn't a good use of the assets that God has entrusted me. Later, I found a better way to rebalance my portfolio: Donate the stocks to my church or nonprofit organizations of my choice.

To some of you who don't usually itemize but give regularly, please consider setting up a donor-derived charitable fund and make a large sum of donations, and you'll receive a tax deduction in the current year. You can then donate out of that fund over time in the next few years.

Additional Notes on Execution.

First, to trade options, you'll need to open a brokerage margin account. With a margin account, you can borrow money to invest in stocks. But please don't borrow any money for your investment. Only invest in the stock market when you have extra, dispensable cash.

Second, I mentioned my professors' comments in an early chapter (Chapter 10) and would like to reiterate it: The US market is very efficient. When a piece of news reaches you, likely most people have already learned about it. Thus, don't believe what others tell you about which stock or option to trade. Do your research and draw your own conclusion. You can read and study what others have to say about your chosen stock/option of interest. Yet take those opinions with a grain of salt.

Third, remember my MBA professor's other advice? At any given time, the pool of money is fixed. When one person loses money, it goes to someone else. If you want to make money, figure out who constantly loses money and do the opposite.

Trading option is trickier than stocks because of the time element. As you buy a stock, you own a piece of that company, and your ownership won't expire until you decide to sell. Options are different because it's not ownership but a contract. When the time is up, the option becomes useless.

Many online sites advertise you can achieve a weekly return of 5% by trading options (mainly from buying them). Yet, according to the stock platform Etoro, 80% of day traders lose money over the course of a year with a median loss of 36.3%. The Wall Street and other sources estimate that 90% of investors lose money buying options.

It's a fact that most people who buy options lose the premium at the expiration of the contract. To make money, do the opposite and sell options.

Fourthly, don't be tempted to sell naked options (i.e., selling a call option without owning the shares, or selling a put option without cash to fulfill the obligation at the option's expiration). It's against the principle of balancing risks and returns.

Even though different option trading strategies (e.g., butterfly spread, straddle...) look alluring, I stick to my approach and use options as a tool to buy and sell stocks. Thus, for put options, I set aside cash in preparation to purchase the stock of interest should its price fall below the strike price in my sold option. And I only sell covered calls (i.e., selling call options on the stocks I own).

I remember one time I shared my tips with someone at church, and a month later, he reported back to me. "Your strategy doesn't work. I was forced to borrow money to buy 1000 shares of XXX stock."

I replied, "I've never borrowed money to buy stocks."

The same individual later made another mistake. "I followed your strategy and sold three contracts of puts to buy ZZZ stocks. Guess what? I'm now stuck with 300 worthless shares."

I challenged him. "Did you research ZZZ and concluded you truly wanted to own a piece of the company for the long run?"

He scratched his head. "A friend told me ZZZ just discovered a big gold mine in Africa. I thought it was a good bet."

Well, don't bet. Do your analysis and be a trustworthy steward of whatever God has entrusted to you.

Chapter 14: Interest Rate and the Stock Market

For 20+ years, putting money in the bank wasn't a good investment strategy because the interest rate was so low. Where else to invest? Trying to strike a risk-return balance wasn't easy. I developed my own method of selling puts to buy stocks and selling calls to sell stocks (see Chapter 13). In doing so, I garnered a decent return on my investment.

In early 2022, the situation changed because the Federal Reserve Bank started to raise the interest rate. The discussion surrounding how central banks employ interest rates to control inflation is a topic worthy of its own exploration, but it is beyond the scope of this article.

As the interest rate rises, the stock market becomes more volatile and the stock prices tend to decrease. Several friends have requested an explanation from me. Here are a few notable reasons that I would like to outline:

1. Cost of borrowing: When interest rates are high, borrowing costs for companies increase. This results in decreased expansion, leading to decreased corporate profits and lower stock prices. Higher interest rates also lure investors to withdraw from the stock market and invest in fixed-income assets like bonds or CDs.

2. Discounted cash flows: Stock valuations rely on the concept of discounted cash flows. When interest rates rise, the discount rate used to calculate the present value of future cash flows also increases. This causes the value of future cash flows to decrease, leading to lower stock prices.

3. Alternative investment options: As mentioned above, when interest rates are high, fixed-income investments become more appealing, and investors may shift money out of stocks into bonds or other fixed-income assets, leading to a decrease in stock prices.

4. Consumer spending and borrowing: Higher interest rates also make it more expensive for people to borrow money, which can limit their ability to make big purchases, such as homes or cars. This can impact consumer spending and business revenues, leading to lower stock prices.

5. Currency exchange rates: Higher interest rates often attract foreign investors seeking higher returns, which will result in a stronger domestic currency. A stronger currency can make exports more expensive and less competitive, which negatively impact the earnings of companies with significant international exposure, leading to lower stock prices.

Can you think of other links between the interest rate and the stock market? Your input will be much appreciated.

Please note that the relationship between interest rates and the stock market is not straightforward. Other factors, such as market sentiment, international events (e.g., wars), and policy decisions, can also influence stock prices. Moreover, different sectors of the stock market may respond differently to changes in interest rates. Therefore, please conduct thorough research before making investment decisions.

Personally, I tend to capitalize on market fluctuations. In the event that the stock market continues to decline, I may consider gradually expanding my equity portfolio by selling put options to acquire additional stocks.

Chapter 15: Asset Allocation and Real Estate

Don't put all your eggs in one basket.

We've all heard this proverb. What's the philosophy behind it? Minimize the risk of losing all you have.

Asset allocation aims to balance risk and reward by placing your hard-earned eggs into different baskets. No simple formula exists for every individual because each of us has different goals, risk tolerance, and investment horizons. For me, I'm willing to take risks for higher returns as long as the investments don't disturb my sleep at night, and I still have peace of mind day in and day out.

The three main asset classes—equities, fixed-income, and cash and equivalents—have different levels of risk and return. In general, the higher the risk, the better the return.

If you need $20,000 for a new car next year, you probably shouldn't put the money into the stock market. Even though the bank interest rate is low, at least by the time you need money for the purchase, you'll have it.

This simple example illustrates the key point: Analyze your current and future situation carefully and put together the investment strategy accordingly.

Of course, nobody can predict the future. The interest rate may go up or down, and stocks will fluctuate. When the interest rate rises, the attractiveness of growth equities decreases. Difficult to win, right?

Ultimately, human lives are in God's hands. Our responsibility is to project and manage.

Numerous books and online articles provide excellent advice about asset allocation: setting aside cash for emergencies, the 60/40 (60% equities/40% bonds) formula, etc. So, I won't delve into the details of those practices. Instead, I'll share how I allocated money to real estate after the collapse of the housing market in 2008.

Buy low and sell high.

We attempt that goal for stocks and other investments as well. But how does one know something has hit its bottom price?

There is no sure way to catch the lowest point. Yet, when the market spirals downward, and everybody is getting out, it's a clear sign to take action.

I watched the burst of the housing bubble with great interest. In late 2009, I checked our bank's interest rate and told Ken, "This is our once-in-a-lifetime opportunity. I think we can have a better return by putting money into real estate."

During a business trip to San Francisco, I checked Zillow.com and noticed a bank-owned house in the East Bay listed for $260,000. A few years ago, the house had sold for $580,000.

I called a broker friend, and we toured the house in the evening. Within a month, we took out a home equity loan against our primary residence and purchased the place.

Back in Chicago, we found a bank-owned condo listed for $140,000. I asked our broker to make a cash offer of $94,000, and the bank accepted it.

In 2010 alone, we bought four rental properties.

For sure, being a landlord is hard work, and it's not for everyone. We hired property managers to maintain the rental properties for us. The reward was that the annual return, after expenses, was better than the bank interest rate. Furthermore, once the housing market stabilized, all the houses appreciated substantially.

That East Bay house in California? Since its value increased so much, we donated it to a Charitable Remainder Trust (see Chapter 17 for more information) to manage our tax liability.

Maybe another bubble of some sort will happen soon and provide an opportunity for one more serious asset allocation.

Chapter 16: Entrepreneurship

Do you ever dream of becoming your own boss so that you can plan your schedule and earn a decent income?

An article by Dragomir Simovic published on July 28, 2022, shows the following statistics:

* Ninety percent of new American billionaires are self-made.
* In 2016, 25 million Americans were starting or already running their businesses.
* The number one reason businesses fail? Lack of a market need for the product.
* Forty-six percent of small business entrepreneurs are between the ages of 41 and 56.
* There are 582 million entrepreneurs in the world.
* Twenty percent of small businesses fail within the first year.

Studies show middle-aged men start the most successful businesses.

Type "entrepreneurship" in the Amazon search box and over 60,000 books will pop up. Rather than replicate those books, I would like to share my experiences.

Stage 1: Planning

The idea of starting my own biotech enterprise came to me when my former employer canceled my project and moved me to a different department. I'd invested a few years of my life in developing new drugs for complications associated with chronic kidney disease and truly believed our effort would eventually help many patients. Then, my company got out of the kidney disease drug sector.

Since I'd taken part in extensive marketing research conducted by the giant pharmaceutical firm where I used to work, I understood the market and competition. I also kept myself well informed about the cost, risks, and challenges of developing a new drug (see Chapter 8 for the five steps involved in bringing a new prescription drug to patients).

I let my idea sit for two years. After many prayers, I put together a business plan and resigned from my job.

Stage 2: Launch

The first step, an easy one, was to incorporate my company.

The much more difficult next step was to secure funding. Back then, we had intangible assets such as ideas, know-how, and experience. But we didn't have patents or anything tangible to attract investors. Through my professional connections, I found several angel investors (wealthy private investors who finance small business ventures in exchange for equity) who shared my ideology. With a $600,000 fund, we set up a lab to start preclinical research.

Stage 3: Move Forward and Maintain

Anyone who has ever worked in the biotech sector will appreciate the fact about how fast research burns cash. We pinched pennies. Still, the initial fund evaporated in less than a year. Fortunately, our first few compounds all tested positive. With the data, we applied for the NIH SBIR (National Institutes of Health Small Business Innovation Research) grants.

To make a long story short, we received six NIH grants and raised two more rounds of funds from investors. The money allowed us to bring our compounds into clinical studies.

Stage 4: Exit

Ten years later, some of our original investors grew restless. When would they see a return on their investment?

We had outstanding data from a clinical study on ten hemodialysis patients. The next step required about $20 million to evaluate the compound in 200 more patients. Would we manage to find the money?

After numerous discussions, our board reached a decision and sold the program to a venture capital firm. Instead of raking in over $200 million with data from a Phase II clinical study, we sold it for about ten times less with the existing data.

Our original investors were well pleased because they received more than a ten-fold return.

The example from my own story is to warn you that, if you are interested in becoming an entrepreneur, please research the four stages described above carefully before you quit your job.

You must estimate the net difference in your income between the current job vs. your new endeavor. In my case, my biotech venture paid me options instead of cash until we received the NIH grants. I prepared for it during the planning process, and our family lived on my husband's income and our investment earnings for a few years.

Another important part of the planning is to analyze the breakeven point of the operations in your new business. Don't be overly optimistic about your potential gain and underestimate the costs and risks. Since it's notoriously difficult to conduct this analysis in the biotech industry, I told all our investors that there was a >95% chance that their money would go down the drain.

Last but not least, never start a business with zero or little experience in the relevant industry. For an entrepreneur, both training and know-how are absolutely crucial. Without my technical background and years of experiences in developing new drugs, my small company would not have attracted the interest of angel investors.

Chapter 17: Retirement and Estate Planning

Nowadays, the term "aging gracefully" seems popular among baby boomers. It could mean "showing signs of growing old, but still moving forward." To me, instead of lamenting about entering the Medicare age, I consider it God's blessing that I still hang around. Many of my friends didn't get the luxury of growing old.

One of my husband's popular seminars is entitled "Love them once more," a tongue-in-cheek presentation on how to manage the last leg of your life so you don't impose unnecessary burdens on your loved ones. The following are some key points.

Purpose in Retirement.

If you type "retirement" in the Amazon search box, you'll find over 70,000 results. How to keep your savings on track, when to collect social security, and what to do for health care... From *Retirement Planning Guide* to *1001 Fun Things to Do in Retirement*, you can take your pick from numerous excellent books.

I won't reinvent the wheel here, but rather share our personal experiences.

We all look forward to the day when we don't have to report to the office and can travel year-round.

And, for us, that day finally arrived.

For the first time in a long while, my husband, Ken, didn't have to follow a tight schedule. Every day felt the same. Fridays no longer brought excitement. A long weekend? What are you talking about? All weekends were too long for him.

His calendar contained no commitments, but also no structure.

After two extended vacations, boredom set in. He needed something to do.

No, we can't travel nonstop like the gentleman we met on our last cruise who spent 26 weeks on the same ship. It would drive us nuts.

Should Ken sign up for more volunteer work? He didn't want to find random activities to kill time. He needed purpose and direction—a new assignment from the Lord so that he could continue to serve in His kingdom.

One of our friends took early retirement and became a missionary in a foreign country.

That was a possibility, but there were many more.

After some seeking, Ken discovered what the Lord wanted him to do.

Yet, everyone is distinct in his or her own way. The key is to pray about it and let the Holy Spirit guide you into your personalized new adventure.

Powers of Attorney (POA), Long-term Care Insurance, and Revocable Living Trust.

If I am fortunate enough, I may reach an age in which my brain no longer functions well. I'll need another person to make major decisions for me. That's when a POA comes into play.

A POA is a legal document that allows another person to make financial or medical decisions for us. In general, we'll need two POAs, one for finances and the other for healthcare. There are some nuances about POAs. You can easily find more information through an online search.

Should I purchase a long-term care insurance policy? Is it worth it? According to the Administration for Community Living, a 65-year-old person has a 70% chance of needing some type of long-term care in the near future. In 2021, the median annual cost of a home health aide was $61,776, and that of a private room in a nursing home was $108,405. If you are super-rich or very poor, don't worry about it. However, for most of us, buying a policy is a wise decision. Like medical insurance policies, you should do it while you're still healthy.

If you start early, you pay premiums over a longer period, but the rate is cheaper and locked in for life.

What about setting up a revocable living trust?

Revocable living trusts, as the name indicates, can be changed over time. They're useful to avoid probate, minimize estate taxes, and protect the privacy of you and your beneficiaries. However, the drawback is that you must hire an attorney to draw up the document and you also need to monitor it on an annual basis and make adjustments as needed. Moreover, you must designate beneficiaries on your retirement accounts and establish transfer-on-death provisions for all non-retirement accounts.

The aforementioned paragraphs aren't meant to give you all the information you need but to prompt you to conduct more research on the subjects.

Charitable Remainder Trusts (CRTs).

I mentioned in a previous chapter (<u>Chapter 15</u>) that I picked up a rental property in the San Francisco East Bay when the housing bubble burst. After my husband retired, we decided to sell that house to retrench our investment in real estate.

There was one serious problem. That house's value increased so much that, if we sold it outright, the tax liability was unbearable.

During that period, we prayed about it on a daily basis. By chance, I happened upon an article about Charitable Remainder Trust (CRT), which I wasn't familiar with. After more research, we considered it as God's answer to our prayer regarding the East Bay house.

What is a CRT? Here is the definition from Wikipedia:

"A Charitable Remainder Annuity Trust (CRAT) is a Planned Giving vehicle that entails a donor placing a major gift of cash or property into a trust. The trust then pays a fixed amount of income each year to the donor or the donor's specified beneficiary. When the donor dies, the remainder of the trust is transferred to the charity. Charitable trusts such as a CRAT require a trustee. Sometimes the charity is named as trustee, other times it is a third party, such as an attorney, a bank, or a financial advisor."

However, the information on Wikipedia isn't 100% accurate. In our case, we set up a CRT for 20 years, which means that the remainder of the trust is transferred to our chosen charity at the end of 20 years, regardless of whether we are still alive. What happens if we die during the CRT duration? Then it automatically goes into our revocable living trust (see above). Moreover, instead of naming someone as a trustee, my husband and I serve as the trustees for our CRT.

Please note that a CRT is irrevocable and complex. You must involve a good lawyer to have it done right. Through the charitable organization we chose, we got in touch with an outstanding Christian attorney who guided us through the entire process.

More About Estate Planning.

The following paragraph is from a friend of ours, Ronald Tolleru, who serves as the Director of Planned Giving and Special Gifts at Trinity International University.

"The primary objective of estate planning is to ensure that your wealth or stuff reaches the persons and organizations you intend for it to reach, at the time and in the form you desire. The secondary objective is to plan the transfer to minimize taxes and other expenses."

Yet, a majority of Americans do not think about estate planning. After a lifetime of working and accumulating an estate, in the end, most people leave the decision of how to depose their properties after death to the state law.

As I emphasized again and again in previous chapters, we, as Christians, should consider everything entrusted to us as temporary. Estate planning is an important step in our effort to be good managers for God and to invest in eternity.

So, as we age, we do what we need to do. Set worries aside and look heavenward.

Chapter 18: Conclusion

One million—1,000,000—symbolizes your life.

With the number **One** intact, all the opportunities become available and achievable.

Remember: Our health is the number **One** that is followed by many zeros. Without that **One**, all those zeros amount to nothing.

I mentioned previously that health, wealth, and relationships intertwine, and it is difficult to single any of them out. As a Christian entrepreneur, to decipher the intimate links between health, finances, and relationships has been my lifelong quest.

One area that I haven't addressed in this booklet is relationships. I left it out on purpose, for it requires an entire book on its own.

My husband and I fit the theory of "opposites attract." He is a night owl, and I'm an early bird. He, a type B personality with a relaxed, patient, and easy-going nature, does not become stressed when he fails to reach his objectives. I, on the other hand, a typical type A, strive toward my goals with a constant sense of urgency at an expense of a balanced life.

During our 40+ years of a wonderful marriage, how did God work in us so that we not only get along well but also help each other achieve equilibrium in body, money, and marriage?

With the Lord's mercy, I hope to share more of my life with you in my next booklet. Meanwhile, I would love to hear your story and your ideas about health, wealth, and relationships. Please drop me a note anytime at the "Leave Comments" page of my website (www.ruthforchrist.com). I welcome guest writers as well.

***

Action Plan: Develop Your Action Plan. An example is shown below. Use the same format for your other action plans to improve your health and finances.

Purpose: To form a habit of exercise every day
Goal: Achieve a visible/measurable change in six months
Evaluation Process: Check weekly to see if your new habit sticks.
Evidence of Success: After six months, check to see if you've made a visible/measurable change in your goal (e.g., exercise every day, lose weight...)
Results/Accomplishments:

Timeline	Things to Do	Support
Step 1 (Week 1):	Write what you want your health to look like.	Go over your list with someone you trust.
Step 2 (Week 2):	Examine your daily routines and identify one "habit loop"—the cue, the routine, and the reward.	Review Chapter 3.
Step 3 (Week 3):	Add an easy-to-do exercise (e.g., ten sit-ups) to your routine without changing the cue and reward.	Share your newly modified routine with your trusted friend.
Step 4 (Weeks 4-7):	Keep up the good work.	Share your progress with your friend at least once a week.
Step 5 (Week 8):	Add another easy-to-do exercise to your routine (e.g., stretching for three minutes).	Share your newly modified routine with your trusted friend.
Week 9 and onward:	Repeat Steps 1-5 until you achieve your goal.	Enjoy the new you.

A Note from the Author

Hello and thank you for sharing this journey with me. If you like the book and have a moment to spare, I would appreciate a short review. Thank you for your help.

About the Author

Wuwong spent twenty-one years as a scientist and then as a marketing manager for a global pharmaceutical company. Then she and her friends founded a biotech company (www.vidasym.com) with a focus on developing new drugs targeting chronic kidney disease. As the company's president, chief scientific officer, and chief financial officer, she successfully raised more than 20 million dollars for Vidasym from angel investors, the National Institutes of Health, venture capital firms, and pharmaceutical companies.

Wuwong has published 120+ scientific papers and books (using her legal name, J. R. Wuwong) plus a few non-scientific books/articles (using her pen name, R. F. Whong). Currently, she lives in the Midwest with her husband, a retired pastor. They served at three churches from 1987 to 2020. Their grown son works in a nearby city.

To connect with her, please go to www.ruthforchrist.com.

Check out the author's fiction books under her pen name, R. F. Whong.

Love at the Garden Tomb (Contemporary romance: https://www.amazon.com/dp/B0B8MK77WK).

The Way We Forgive (Women's fiction: https://www.amazon.com/dp/B0BQ5LNLNB).

Blazing China (Family saga: https://www.amazon.com/dp/B0CD9P49HW). Amazon's #1 New Release in Asian Literature.

Detour to Agape (Contemporary romance and a sequel to *Blazing China*: https://www.amazon.com/dp/B0CD9P29GJ)